BY THE SAME AUTHOR*

Poems

DEAD-MAN'S-FALL
   (The Bodley Head 1980)
A SAD PARADISE
   (Lines Review Editions, Macdonald 1990)

Translations

OSIP MANDELSHTAM
Poems chosen and translated by James Greene
   (Elek 1977, Shambhala 1978, Granada 1980, Angel Books 1989, Penguin 1991)
AFANASY FET: I have come to you to greet you
   (with Cynthia Westwood) Angel Books 1982
OLAV H. HAUGE: Don't give me the whole truth
   (with Robin Fulton and Siv Hennum) Anvil 1985
FERNANDO PESSOA: The surprise of being
   (with Clara de Azevedo Mafra) Angel Books 1986
J.-B. PONTALIS: Love of beginnings
   (with Marie-Christine Réguis) Free Association Books 1990

Plays

KILLING TIME IN THE KREMLIN

THE BIN

Translated plays

AMPHITRYON, Kleist

THE AUTHORITIES, Jens Bjørneboe
   (with Siv Hennum)

Uncollected poems and translations of poems have been published in *Argo,
Autistic Barriers in Neurotic Patients* (Frances Tustin), *Bananas, Comparative
Criticism 8,* the *Cumberland Poetry Review, Encounter, Lines Review, Litmus,*
the *London Magazine,* the *London Review of Books,* the *New Review,* the *New
Statesman,* the *New Yorker, Other Poetry, Outposts, Pix 2,* the *Poetry Book Society
Anthology 1989-1990, Poetry Durham, Poetry Ireland Review, PN Review, Poems
from Mary Ward, Poetry Nottingham, Poetry Review, Thames Poetry,* the *Times
Literary Supplement, Verse,* and *Winnicott Studies 2, 3 and 4.*

*This summary doesn't include all prose writings: for example, a paper in the
International Journal of Psychoanalysis (1967 or 1968) now disowned, and others
in *Contemporary Psychoanalysis* and *Free Associations.*

Not prone to ancestor-worship, I nonetheless feel a fondness for Dr Robert Whytt, first physician in Scotland to George III. In 1766 Whytt was borne by horses through the streets of Edinburgh: a public funeral, his reward for the nothingness of death. Two years earlier, he published his *Observations on the Nature, Causes and Cures of Those Disorders which Have Been Commonly Called Nervous, Hypochondriac or Hysteric.* My great-great-great-great-grandfather's remedies for "low spirits", "distress of mind" and "melancholy" consisted of exercise (especially riding), travelling, cold baths, "agreeable company", "a variety of amusements", claret and opium: nothing "medical" here any more than, a century or so later, in the procedures and accoutrements of the prodigious Viennese investigator, a "neurologist" too and one of sense and sensuality: alleviations, in his case, by virtue of nothing but the splendours and miseries of speech and a comfortable couch.

With Irish, Norwegian, Scottish, even English ancestors, I was born in Berlin in 1938, mother-tongue German, babbling, I like to think, in the manner of Georg-Friedrich Händel or lisping the same syllables as Goethe – and, I like to forget, Hitler. Attendance at New College, Oxford and University College, London preceded various rôles in NHS psychiatric hospitals. And, an improbable practitioner, I occupied for a number of years the seat behind the couch.

While Robert Whytt's *pompes funèbres* were wowing the proletariat of Edinburgh, his patrician patients naturally stayed at home in front of fires stoked by obliging flunkeys. Elsewhere, in the next century, William Smith, my great-great-grandfather, made his living as a coal merchant and, with his own small sailing vessel, transported fuel along the Wash. Like him, I've been engaged in transportations, though only from one language to another and in comfort; unlike him, I can't know whether what I do is warming. Any claim that poems, by themselves, cure melancholy or lessen a reader's or writer's cold darknesses is debatable, even if Wordsworth's did for John Stuart Mill. On the other hand, I wouldn't, like Auden, want to assert that poetry makes *nothing* happen. Perhaps – not often – this "nothing" can be as intoxicating as claret or as welcome as a coal-fire or cold bath: momentarily, at any rate.

Whatever the truth, this small bunch of poems is for saying goodbye to those who, over almost fifty years, brought to our walks on Hampstead Heath the *whytt* and warmth of their amiability; and as a fading last floral tribute to others I know who, without medications, minister to distress of mind in all its 57 varieties, mine included, by transforming unnameable *ghosts*, more familiar to the medical-minded as "symptoms", into imaginable "ancestors", so that tongue-tied silences, haunting or annihilating because ineffable, become words and syntax – and, rather than life-sentences, sentences on the side of life: ancestors black-suited, perhaps, but ones who wear, in the end, unfunereal red socks, straw hats, and carnations instead of nothing in their buttonholes: adorned, above all, with *speech*. For me, psychoanalysis is a God that didn't Fail: there are so many things I need to see. – JG

To Ignês Sodré and Nicky Sherrott, in the order in which I had the amazing luck to come to know them: this is for you above all, my ideal imaginary readers.

To Will and Camilla, for my being fortunate enough to become part of your to-me-particularly-significant lives, during the last fifty-four and thirty-six years of mine.

And to two writers, known by me by now for a total of one-hundred-and-twenty-seven years, David Black and John Fuller, whose works I especially admire and whose being around over such a long stretch of time (John and I were at the same school when I was ten) has meant so much to me.

TO THE ULTIMATE PARAMOUR

Twice or thrice had I lov'd thee,
Before I knew thy face or name…

A whirl of dervishes,
disciples of Shaykh Abdullah,
a swirling avenue
of white-blossoming trees,
lookalikes identical as leaves:
under tall brown hats
their brains no longer hot,
they – for now – eschew

desire and singularity.
I, your devotee, do not.
I am like some ancient fox-cub
who, of all the flowerbeds
of lavender, has found
this one to (sh)amble round.

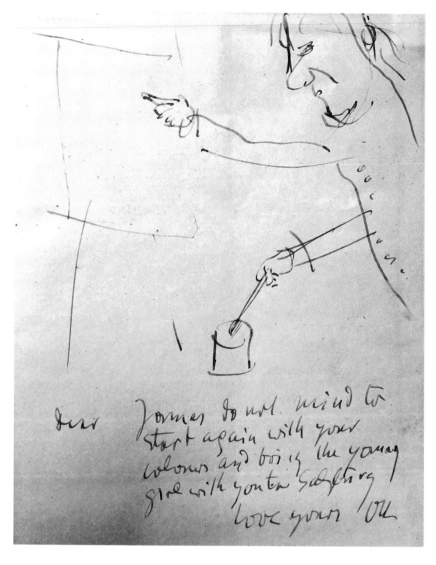

*"Dear James do not mind to start again with your colours and
bring the young girl with you to Salzburg   Love yours OK"*
Courtesy of Fondation Oskar Kokoschka. Date of sketch: 1957.

CONTENTS

TALLER TODAYS

Scraps of aunt Kate's sandwiches
still taunt from glittering beaks.

On sand smooth as peanut butter,
no longer yapping at the getaway

of kleptomaniac or wily gulls,
nor whimpering, one eye shut,

as when the crimson kite crashed,
seagull-sniffing yellow Lego eyes,

with toothy focus, the majestic
pram-imprisoned baby shave

lopsided morsels of moustache.
Charlie's wiggly tongue scrabbles

across vanilla lathered chins
and cheeks, and our aunt Kate

is all-but overheard to murmur:
"A blunted pocket-knife is pointless".

Is her point to do with what is lost,
melting irreparably or shrinking?

*

His latest throne an upturned bucket
trumpeting its melon-yellow, Charles,

our drug-assisted Pope who wears
a cardinal's red bobble-hat, chuckles

while, tipsy not on Sundays only,
he pardons a parent who performs

the everyday miracle of milk.
"Growing up, you see", pointedly

all-knowing Mark remarks, "means
knowing where your daily bread

is buttered". For him, I'm so naive
I'm not worth knowing, but Anna

enrols me as her honorary sister,
though hankering for a real one.

*

Aunt Kate ahead of us with Charlie,
Lego fidgety and shivering,

Anna and I, now hand in hand,
shake the sand from these sandals

and, making light of what is dark,
stride towards… precisely what?…

but, at least, knowing no better,
embrace – up to a point – our paradise,

fun at times, sometimes said to be sad.

HUMPTY'S FALL

Yes, absence
is attack:
your lack
of summonable
cradling arms –

O, for an asylum,
a straitjacket!
I, cracked lunatic,
brain racked,
my mouth

a belfry
devoid of bells
or any sound-track
for my own funeral,
must, plunging down,

die for ever –
a minus, nonplussed.
Screamingly funny,
I know, to see,
(in red not black)

all the King's men
fall over each other
and fail
to put me together again:
fat chance of that

now that I've lost
the power to chortle.
I'm not deaf, though,
to the snort of horses
or the howl of nothingness.

FLOWERS FOR THE FEMALE WARD, 1963

Psychiatrists can recognize madmen by the visible agitation they
display after involuntary commitment. – Karl Kraus

At twenty-five, my first day in this fortress, and I fail to hide
the garrulous bunch of keys I need to get inside.
The inmates must be dangerous – to themselves, not me:

I'm no more harmful than this unforthcoming bumblebee.
Why not bring yellow bouquets of silent-speaking roses,
to be *observed* at least by faces shorn as if of ears and noses?

The tulips here, blood-orange, open-mouthed, are left to stare,
unlooked-at, from the window-boxes those inside ignore.
So many jangling barriers! When I unlock the ultimate interior door

women in night-dresses jostle to pounce on me and paw:
they gasp and moan and jabber, or jerk my jacket-sleeves.
Women of a seraglio? No: pickpockets – sex-starved thieves!

For "treatment", I have chosen one – she's thirty – already here
ten years. She doesn't speak at all and hardly stirs. Oh dear!
Is it so beneficial, for her or me, to be her so-called "therapist"?

I might be less injurious by retreating, like the tenured Trappist
she appears to be, instead of diving in – where angels fear to tread –
as someone far too ignorant to rescue someone far too drowned.

By dusk, already five of this ward's captives dumbly weep
as tulip-coloured bountiful libations coagulate or trickle or seep
from wrists, as if – instructed by such tell-tale stigmata in how

to find asylum in themselves – they want to indicate or show,
or blazon even, the blessings of their god-forsaken lives
dedicated to the overcoming, with the help of stolen knives,

of quasi-crucifixion, agony and tongue-tied pain:
each face a sunflower now, they welcome tears like rain,
not knowing that drought returns and unarticulated pangs are all in vain.

DON'T COME WITH THE WHOLE TRUTH

after Olav Hauge

Don't come with the sea
when I ask for water,
or sky when I thirst for light.

Come with a gleam, a dew, a fleck,
as a bird brings drops from dipping in the sea
and the wind bears specks of salt.

LEARNING TO READ IN A GRAVEYARD

We two somersault, my aunt Kate and I,
 by Albert's burial plot.
Once left for dead on a wheelbarrow, he
 survived that war
and came to life in the graveyard here
 with his red watering-can.

Inscriptions, like the blue veronicas he planted,
 mottle and blotch:
Albert George Sparrow (1897-1969) who died
 to save a ferret.
Our sponge now scrubs the letters back to life,
 black once more

like grandpa's suit, the one he solemnly put on
 when Albert swerved to miss
a nervy diffident family of dithering ferrets
 crossing the road:
Albert, who vexed the verges and the vicar
 and tied his bike

to railings here that warn "Keep off": in case
 the Rev., he said,
tempted to steal, might one day learn to read
 or even be charitable. –
The shriek of brakes. Albert's cycle-clips
 unharmed.

He almost lost his leg and life in the Great War
in which Kate, the same age as him, lost her lover.

A PLACE OF EXECUTION: COUNTY MAYO, 1845

Hooves upside-down, our hinny – progeny of a nag's pizzle
and donkey's hoarse complaisance – is pedalling
to applaud the barley sky, then leaping round her mammy
who squinnies at the water-trough. Years later, chafed by shafts,
stiff-necked, she tries to break out. We try to break her in.

Later still, a vision of potato peelings invades her trance.
A whinny, a cough, a wobble: she scratches an ear,
gulps a flea, then squints, gaping
at inedible sky (pumpkin, lime-green, pomegranate),
scowled at by the turnip-nosed mountain.

A skinny scarecrow, delicate as your own rope of spittle
and pale as a parsnip, you stagger or sprawl, as if just born.
Now ravenous like you, we eat you, scraggy though you are,
charming though you were,
yoked together – as in life – in death: *we* now bow our heads.

CIVIL WAR: THE BATTLE OF THE SLIDE, PARLIAMENT HILL PLAYGROUND

A lone and battlemented daughter
garrisons this look-out tower's platform.
"Come down – you're not yet five!"

Portcullis of hair defends her ears,
a wounding silence flagging up
an unconditional no-surrender.

Not fortified by blunderbuss or schnapps,
I (crestfallen, banner drooped) watch
the dragging of defeated feet – my own –

mount the scaffold's axe-cold one-way stair
to face those lovely to-be-pitied eyes,
my unexonerating executioner's.

WEEKLY SWIMMING CLASS

Scratching their acne, the boys excoriate the blotchiness of girls
who, shivering, already sense they'll never get what they deserve,

although today their eager not-yet-perfect breaststroke is enough,
requiring only frowns of singlemindedness and dizzy verve.

The edifying boys, sperm-squirting mammals when at home in bed
but here less cocksure and more sheepish, hesitantly perve

and, only when the godlike lifeguard's back is turned, wolfishly
horn in, outside the pool, to trip the budding girls who have to swerve

to slip past predators whose twitching feet must, for the moment, serve
as stand-ins on behalf of jumpy tentacles internationally renowned

for their spasmodic jerking, zealous insolence and explosive nerve:
miraculous appliances, these half-cocked water-pistols of the pool.

IN THE UNDERGROUND

Their knees aren't touching, but an upstart
on parade needs to be dismissed, ordered
back to barracks, if he's to get off less
disconcerted by a still-unflopping pennant.
Fourteen: the Age of awkward precipitations
and of blushing! They've met before, but now
she is his father's latest and much younger wife.
Not quite the moment, then, to rise bulgingly –
the train shudders towards Oxford Circus – even if
he were some upstandingly flexible fornicator,

even if *attracted* – so far as he's aware (how far
is that?) he isn't: so, is his upfront effrontery
vibrational purely? Not even "Divinity" at school,
the acrobatics of its tripartite, suicidal God
whose "son" does not abhor ("abhor"?)
a virgin mother's womb, is helping him to feel
less divided, hazardous, at odds, as – red in the face –
he clutches with one hand the dangling strap:
only half of a trapeze, no safety-net in sight.
The *body*, he's discovering, has minds all of its own.

SURPRISE

Some things thrill even when
their meanings be deferred
like murmured conversations
not wholly overheard,

as once (absentmindedly,
perhaps) – is this absurd? –
your hand brushed mine,
its sense or non-sense blurred

in the manner of a rustling tree
whose branches seem unstirred:
accidental – or on purpose…
The tread of some soft bird.

PATRIARCHY'S UPS AND DOWNS

The most mediocre of males feels himself a demi-god as compared with women. – Simone de Beauvoir (1949)

For women, the brief powers of the phallus – the acclaimed instrument of intromission – are only lent or borrowed. Some women still find this hard to acknowledge: as the Very Rev. Thomas Stearns Eliot says in "Four Quartets", quoting either God or Stetson, "Humankind" – or, more precisely, womankind – "cannot bear very much reality". (1980)*

SHE
I may still rustle up a (lacklustre) *fondue*,
if almost in the mood: with finely judged
incompetence, reluctant to distinguish sugar from salt.

HE
I wish to contemplate my own vast alpine range
of intellectual projects and pursuits:
these seminal works exposing lesser-known lacunae

in Lacan, not to mention my own wondrous sequel to
J.J.'s paltry half-unfinished booklet, *Finnegans Wake*:
I, who once had time, intoxicated and fully nude,

as it were, to ski across a mental Switzerland
of lakes and glaciers. But now your blizzard
of dirty plates blocks my view, impedes my progress

and my climb, and I must choke, an aproned skivvy,
under a smirking female killjoy Calvin's cosh.
It isn't fair. Posterity will maledict you.

SHE
If, for you, crevasse and complication preoccupy
your mind to the detriment of any washing-up, why not
join J.J. in, as it were, a Zürich now enriched by Dignitas?

*See Dr. Roger Snoop, Willie Z. Slijper, Dick J. Cockrum Jnr, H. Magniac and Professor Lionel Tyger: *Human Reproduction and ineluctable Evolution.*

HOTEL IN ÅSGÅRDSTRAND, 1888

My great-grandfather Otto never wears
pyjama-bottoms in bed. Upright now,
still naked, he gazes out to sea, inhaling air
as violatingly-agreeable as aquavit.
His wife distracted too, both ignore
the timid tap as Ingun tip-toes in. A tray
with coffee-pot and jam crashes to the floor
and, freckly face a spreading pink, she flees.

Ambushed by a glimpse of tears, Otto
hops into pyjamas kept for show, resumes
his earlier ship-captain's pose, and signals
for my great-grandmother to ring the bell:
Ingun will feel so much better when she sees
that she, mistaken, is only *seeing things.*

REPORT BY DER KAPITÄN FRITZ WIEDEMANN ON HITLER'S SUITABILITY FOR OFFICER TRAINING, 1917

Der Korporal Hitler, conscript, has served under my command
for two years now. As a despatch-runner
he demonstrates germanic courage
when carrying messages to the front line,
fearless under enemy fire and obedient as a little lap-dog.
Indeed, his devotion to me is exemplary
in its (albeit slovenly) slavishness: few soldiers

achieve such unthinking recklessness. His posture
undisciplined and sloppy – he seems unable even
to hold his head up straight – tattered thoughts
tumble out, uninvited, and, when asked a simple question,
he rambles, distracted like someone seeing things.
And he is *vegetarian*. This, in itself, renders him of course
unsuitable to become an officer, his uncarnivorous physique

leaving too much to be desired. In short, experience
informs me, beyond the shadow of a doubt,
that he would be incapable of not ruining, let alone running,
a dogs' home even. He, the kind of *lumpen-soldat*
indispensable as cannon-fodder, shouldn't be promoted:
I need him where he is, close to the front line. Here, if lucky,
he might earn, in a flash, an Iron Cross and early death.

CABARET IN A MUNICH BEER-HALL, 1934: IN THE NAME OF...

On the subject of Hitler, nothing occurs to me. – Karl Kraus

Karl Valentin, in boots far too big, an orange wig
and proletarian cloth-cap and overalls, bolts onto the stage,
shouldering a ladder, running for his life, stumbles and falls;
the ladder shoots across the floor.
Picking his body up, he dusts himself down
and darts a furtive glance behind to address his props,
a golden throne and a gigantic mirror: "Heil… *Rudolf*?"
(Pause.) "Heil… *Littler*?" "*Did someone snigger*?" (Pause.) "*Or snivel*?"

Some chuckle uneasily. Some shudder. And a foreign-correspondent –
he's read *Mein Kampf* and seen inside Dachau for himself –
recalls its dead or empty eyes as well as ancient banishments:
Ovid in exile, weeping buckets by the sea called Black, himself
remembering the shaggy Scythians, their ox-and-bullock waggons,
the march of the barbarians. And Dachau now, less than two years
after its conception and its birth, already named in nursery rhymes
that make the children shiver and their parents shake.

Like a rabbit blinking in the headlights of a wolf's eyes,
Valentin races out, then – shunting those enormous boots of his –
meanders back and shies away again,
mumbling an apologetic stuttered "Heil".
Propping his ladder against the wall, he begins to climb,
his knees buckle and, tears wetting his cheeks, he tumbles down.

Yawning, about to crumple onto the throne, he falters,
then dashes around it dizzily
until it's time, with torch, to search behind.
"Heil… *Bettler*?" (Long pause.) He scratches his head.
"Heil… ?" Striking his heart, he whispers:
"*The name – Gott in Himmler!* I've forgotten the name".

Some of those here who don't dare openly to die of laughter will soon die.

THE NAZIS AND LIPSTICK, BERLIN 1935

War breaks out in wellington boots in a squelchy
and sopping public garden: accosted by two jabbing youths
who swear at her for wearing lipstick, outraged Helga –

her friend recounts – lashes these incorruptible defenders
of their Fatherland with her eighteen-year-old tongue:
my mother, just married, has discovered make-up.

Expecting subservience, the youths scuttle off, kicking
the gravel, red in the face, scorched by her scarlet mouth:
two wholesome Nazi thugs meet their muddy Waterloo.

Helga could have said: Hitler's just-appointed Adjutant
has, like a movie-star or salivating zeiss-eyed Zeus,
spotted her in a fashionable outdoor café and, faced

with the red-hot lips the youths abhor, Captain Wiedemann,
in spite of noticing she's married (and to whom) and less
than half his age, is still bombarding her with compliments

and roses, smitten by that Aryan armoury of auburn hair,
blue eyes and white translucent skin, if not her trenchant tongue.
But here, on such a battlefield, his chivalry isn't ideal:

at eighteen my mother can draw blood. And shouldn't, instead,
her formidable artillery of crimson lips have led him to retreat,
like the virtuous bullies, tail limp between his booted legs?

IN 1940 POLICE CONSTABLE SAVAGE OF THE DORSETSHIRE CONSTABULARY SEES A SIGHT

On Chesil beach few corpses come to rest
to mar the revelry at "The Dolphin Arms".
But today a charred pilot in a green field
sunbathes, indifferent to the Luftwaffe
of midges constituting his guard of honour.
Henry Savage, sun-dazed, fumbling
over dizzy buttons, lays bare a powder-puff,
lipsticks, and pink silk underclothes.

He peers, helmet dripping sweat, averts
his eyes and straightens up, his cheeks
a scarlet blaze, perhaps already dreaming
of "The Dolphin's" barmaid, whose eyes
arrested his when scolding him (*fancies
he's the Pope, must be the uniform...*)
so charmingly for shyly spilling loose coins
onto her shiny and undegenerate counter.

THE RESIDENT ALIENS

My couch doesn't have room for you to loll for ever.
Siesta-time. A gatecrasher snubs me on the stairs, to claim
a couch I thought was mine: displaced, by the bombastic moth.

A cat swings by one day and now turns up at six each morning.
He strokes and plucks and leaps around my ball of string,
borrowed without asking. O unhinged harpist, tie yourself in knots.

The ginger mouse, spying on the cat's Houdini-variations,
nimbles out, heart throbbing, wet nostrils twitching
for a bite of pecorino – or a passport.

A gawky daddy-longlegs loiters in my bath.
Should I "rescue" him or leave him in possession?
Will it help his skeletal self-confidence to escape *without* my help?
The sides of baths are sheer: he'd have to exit via the plug-hole –
from where, for all I know, he may have strolled.

How unfathomable and *déracinés* cats are.
And *all* my fellow-refugees, guilty of seditious loyalty
to some foreign paleolithic jurisdiction's *præmunire*.

I entertain vast dreams of deportation. But how, where to?
And I – deprived of funeral cortège when I come to die?
But – loopy cat, couch-happy moth, asylum-seeking mouse
and gangling daddy-longlegs – *are* you better than nothing? You
wouldn't mourn for me – nor I for you. No protocols of loss.

Weeks of non-attendance, and the cat – "my" cat, the nameless one –
has vanished for good. And grief, that unanticipated émigré,
moves in, with all its soggy luggage. The cross-eyed mouse

can now luxuriate in rococo reveries of risk-free crumbs.
And, yes – why not? – welcome, moth. Perhaps. But don't presume:
my couch does not have room for you to loll for ever.

THE CART

after Milosz

Over the fields we bounce and bump.
The sky is black, a redwing startles.
You point: a hare, pelting across our path.

Years pass. You and the hare are dead.

My love, where are they? – The gleam,
the hand, the sprinting hare. The cart
creaks and rattles over ruts and frozen clods.

FROM THE ANATOMY OFFICE: AFTER LIFE

Uprooted by being born, I couldn't do better
than die, if then I might lie down with Lady Sudeley
in a lemony orchard with its sting of strawberry.

Eyes wrapped in muslin bandages, corpse
transplanted to dissection-rooms, the music here
a whirr of drills, a muffled scrape of scalpels:

the unused parts of "me" a scatter of bright ashes –
nameless now but rooted and belonging (fabulous,
if true) – are branching out as pink-striped apples

dumbfounded in an orchard-clearing, a blaze
of Blenheim Oranges or Russets of Egremont
with (imagine!) an otherworldly damson flavour.

No more unlikely than a dead "god" rising from a tomb.

A KIND OF LIFE AND AFTERLIFE: DON MANUEL OSORIO MANRIQUE DE ZUÑIGA PAINTED BY FRANCISCO DE GOYA Y LUCIENTES IN 1788

In red silk suit, a bad-tempered – let us say – ungovernable nurse-maid
is out of sight while he is clutching a flimsy-looking string attached

to his pet magpie on the floor, gawked at by a cat with shiny bulging eyes
spied on by two other cats lurking in the shadows and loitering with intent,

all held in mind by one who couldn't credit any creator superior
to himself who might be capable of preserving every sparrow, let alone –

unless with oil on canvas – all his seven sprogs, one surviving still
when he no longer is, by when our Manuel, nearly eight, has swapped

a cage of silk for one of lead: those leaping claws have pounced. And yet –
and yet – so long as onlookers can gaze transfixed, Manuel lives sadly on.

BEGINNINGS

There is a crack a crack in everything / That's how the light gets in.
– Leonard Cohen

One leg on the mat, my mama
steps out, her other limb cut short
by the angle of the bath. Tufts
of red moustache, above a pursed mouth
of snipped dismemberment, ravish

the bathtub-white and greet me
like an unabashing affidavit.
So this archaic slithery trench
is my scooped-out, dank, labial,
adventitious, heavenly source.

Springtime on the earth for now:
a leaf-encrusted pond, the nibbling
slime-fresh tench breeding underneath,
whose ice, so transiently, supports
a skater's elated precarious weight.

SO, GOODBYE

Splashing through this stream, the day so hot,
I'm leaping, no longer lugubrious, almost jaunty.
I saw a pheasant, took aim, and shot:
the church-tower bell is ringing now throughout the valley

emptied by Black Death – my arrow hit the sun-lit distant bell.
A bear, who must have sheltered there
all winter, honey-coloured ecclesiastical animal,
takes one look at me, lopes off, bell ringing still, Spring in his ears.

NOTES

On the page to do with myself I've borrowed the "ghost" and "ancestor" formulation or image from Hans Loewald, via Jonathan Lear; I hope I'm using it in more or less the sense they intended.

Page 10, *Humpty's fall*: "… Hurled headlong from the ethereal sky / With hideous ruin and combustion down…" – *Paradise Lost*

Page 14: my Irish ancestors, in mediaeval times, were Gaelic-speaking churls or serfs, in what is now County Down: not *Anglo*-Irish.

Page 18: *Surprise* sprouts, very much truncated, from a poem by Fernando Pessoa, *Foi um momento*: from *The Surprise of Being*, Angel Books, 1986, translated with the help of Clara de Azevedo Mafra.

Pages 21 and 23: Captain Fritz Wiedemann (1891-1970): Hitler's Commanding Officer during the First World War and, when Hitler was recommended for officer training, Wiedemann objected on the grounds that the Corporal lacked leadership qualities. (This turned out, of course, to be both right and wrong.) Presumably Hitler never knew that Wiedemann had blocked his promotion: in any case, in 1935 the former Captain was appointed, in a curious reversal of rôles, Hitler's Personal Adjutant at the Reich Chancellery.

Page 22: Karl Valentin (1882-1948): satirical comedian, cabaret performer, clown and film actor, he was, like Chaplin, very much admired by, and an important influence on, Brecht.

Page 26: the Milosz poem is an early poem of his entitled – in his own translation – *Encounter*: my thanks to Ora Dresner for essential help with the Polish and for being the friend everyone needs but few can find. As, too, to Siv Hennum with Olav Hauge's Norwegian (page 12), our version first published in *Don't give me the whole truth* (Anvil, 1985), in which the majority of the translations are by Robin Fulton.

SEEING THINGS
JAMES GREENE

First published in Great Britain by
Golden Hare in 2023

Copyright © The author 2023

The author asserts the moral right to be
identified as the author of this work

A catalogue record for this book is
available from the British Library

ISBN 978 1 8384 0654 7

Designed by James Brook,
www.jamesbrook.net

Printed and bound in Great Britain
by Gomer Press, Wales

Golden Hare
68 St Stephen Street,
Edinburgh EH3 5AQ
Scotland,
United Kingdom

*Find out more about Golden Hare
from www.goldenharebooks.com*

ACKNOWLEDGEMENTS

I want to acknowledge the bountifulness of Eileen Gunn and the Royal Literary
Fund. Anybody requiring a virtual PA/Secretary need look no further than
Mae Walsh of Outsource HQ at hq@outsourcehq.net, who combines expertise
with exceptional good humour and perfect charm; this bunch of poems owes
far more to her than I could ever say. For printing, copying, binding and banter
I'm indebted to all at Printline, London NW3: Alina, Harry, Bill, and Chirag. My
thanks to Adrian Chapman for undertaking the thankless task of proof-reading.
I've enjoyed the blunt comments of sharp and sensitive friends, for instance David
(D.M.) Black and John Fuller. Nicky Sherrott, the most perceptive editor anyone
could wish for, has accompanied these poems all the way and, recently, their
progress towards publication. Innumerable thanks are also due to Colin Falck
for another long friendship, our exchange of poems and his Thurlow Road Poetry
Workshop, as well as to the much-missed, wonderful and ever-lucid John Torrance.
Jane Duran's help has been invaluable. I'm much indebted to Mark Jones for his
unerring tact and discernment, his various skills as Golden Hare's ring-master,
and not least for his choice of James Brook, this pamphlet's subtle, reflective and
inspiring designer. Finally, I salute Robin Leanse: he and I, having already shared
many hours on Hampstead Heath, now share the same publisher; it's a pleasure to
follow in his intense and delightful footsteps.